THE
CAMPAIGN

Good News for a Partisan World

Michael Hudson

ISBN 978-1-0980-1361-5 (paperback)
ISBN 978-1-0980-1362-2 (digital)

Christian Faith Publishing, Inc.
832 Park Avenue
Meadville, PA 16335
www.christianfaithpublishing.com

Printed in the United States of America

For my mother,
whose prayers led me to vote,
and
for my wife,
whose encouragement keeps me on the campaign trail

CONTENTS

INTRODUCTION

"This Just in: Jesus Is Still Lord."

That was the message on our church sign Wednesday, November 9, 2016. It was the day after the most surprising presidential election in American history.

Needless to say I received an e-mail from someone (not a member of our church) who had seen the sign and was upset. She assumed the sign meant that God had answered our prayers with the results and we were gloating. I told her that I could see how she could interpret our sign in that fashion, but I assured her that is not what it meant.

She was angry, angry at the results of the election, angry at the church for being "involved," angry that people she considered evil had won and understandably so. She, like so many others, had their hopes crushed. Their faith in a good future appeared to be ripped out from under them. And while some may have felt that the election results were an answer from God, others couldn't believe God would allow such a thing to happen.

Both political parties today think they are good and the other is evil. (I don't use that term lightly.) Both sides see no common ground and that they have a moral imperative to resist anything the other does. I understand people have different views on issues—that's why we have different political parties—but the absolute lines that have been drawn between them and the vitriol that now exists is at a dangerous level. It is a powder keg waiting for a spark.

How did we get to such a place?

I am convinced that the reason so many people on both sides are so polarized when it comes to politics is because both sides, ironically, have something fundamental in common. Both sides are looking for a leader who will provide peace, security, justice, and prosperity. In short, everyone is looking for a Savior. And political campaigns promise them one.

As long as people have been able to choose their leaders, those leaders promise what the people want. So we get campaign slogans like:

"Vote Yourself a Farm" from Abraham Lincoln in 1860, "Patriotism, Protection, and Prosperity" from William McKinnley in 1896, and then for re-election in 1900 "A Full Dinner Pail."

In 1916 Woodrow Wilson's slogan was "He Kept Us Out Of War." After Wilson's slogan was short-lived because of World War I, Warren Harding promised a "Return to Normalcy" in 1920. Before the Stock Market Crash and Great Depression, Herbert Hoover promised in 1928 "A Chicken in Every Pot and a Car in Every Garage." More recently in 2008, we had Barrack Obama promise "Hope" and "Change We Can Believe In." And, of course, Donald Trump promised to "Make America Great Again."

So people cling with fierce loyalty to their saviors and political parties because that is where they have put their trust for hope and happiness, significance and security. But doing so is nothing but good ole' fashioned idolatry. Has any candidate ever been able to deliver on their campaign slogan? These promises and politicians will always leave us empty, frustrated, angry, and unfulfilled—especially when they lose the election. Idols do that. You would think we would have learned that lesson by now.

Psalm 118:8–9 gives us some ancient advice that we would be wise to heed today. *"It is better to take refuge in the Lord than to trust in man. It is better to take refuge in the Lord than to trust in princes."* The temptation to put our trust in our politicians and political parties is great. After all, there have been some great men and women who have run for office and done good things. Yet, even so, we have an expectation that one day someone will come along who can really fix things. We keep waiting for that day.

But what if that day has already come? What if that candidate has already come on the scene? What if someone ran for the highest office and was able to keep his campaign promises? Would you vote for that person? What would that campaign look like? Turns out, it wouldn't look much different than the campaigns today.

The Gospel of Mark can be read like a political campaign. Read through this lens, Mark comes complete with everything you need for a high-stakes contest. It has a reform candidate, primaries, slogans, campaign stops in different towns, grassroots support, campaign promises, a party platform, opposition from the establishment, debates, false accusations, bribes, election eve sabotage, an assassination, and of course, a vote.

You might be thinking to yourself, "Why read Mark's Gospel like a campaign when most people believe religion and politics should be kept separate?" For starters, everything that happened in the Gospel of Mark and to Jesus happened in a highly politicized context. Everyone who heard Him, heard Him with political ears. He used kingdom language deliberately. And He wasn't talking about a spiritual kingdom in the sweet bye and bye. Indeed, if you miss the political context, you miss much of what Jesus is doing and saying. Perhaps a look at a classic "Christmas" passage may give you a taste of what I am talking about. See if you can find any political references in it.

"For to us a child is born, to us a son is given, and the government will be upon his shoulders. And he will be called Wonderful Counselor, Mighty God, Everlasting Father, Prince of Peace. Of the increase of his government and peace there will be no end. He will reign on David's throne and over his kingdom, establishing and upholding it with justice and righteousness from that time on and forever. The zeal of the Lord Almighty will accomplish this." (Isa. 9:6–7)

Another reason to have a campaign in mind as you read Mark is that there is nothing new under the sun. What you see in contemporary campaigns has been going on for thousands of years. Politics has always been a major factor in life. Jesus is not afraid to step into the fray, answer questions, and lay it all on the line. After all, hope and change are not recent issues.

Also, we have free will to love God or reject Him. So Jesus campaigns for our trust, our love, and our allegiance. Then He gives us a choice—a vote. He asks, *"Who do you say that I am?"* Every person on the planet gets a vote.

But perhaps the biggest reason to look at the Gospel of Mark like a political campaign is, as E. Stanley Jones said, "There is no place where Jesus is out of place." Many in our culture believe the church has no place in the political arena. They say Jesus proclaims a spiritual kingdom. But Jesus isn't Lord of just heaven. He is Lord of heaven and earth. Theologian Abraham Kuyper famously wrote, "There is not a square inch in the whole domain of human existence over which Christ, who is Sovereign over all, does not cry: 'Mine!'" Jesus is not afraid of the political arena, but the political arena may well be afraid of Him.

I invite you to read the Gospel of Mark along with this book. The Scripture references are listed at the beginning of each chapter. I use the New International Version 84. All Scripture passages are italicized.

I told my congregation weeks before the 2016 election that no matter who won, the sign out front would read, "This Just in: Jesus Is Still Lord." Let's find out why.

THE PRIMARIES

***

Mark 1:14–8:26

I do not know if the people of the United States would
vote for superior men if they ran for office, but there
can be no doubt that such men do not run.

—Alexis de Tocqueville

THE ANNOUNCEMENT

Mark 1:1–11

I'm Al Gore. I used to be the next president
of the United States of America.
　　　　　　　　　—Al Gore, *An Inconvenient Truth*

If you run for office, you have to begin your campaign with a big splash. Candidates stage the whole event. Endorsements, cheering crowds, flags, decorations, and campaign signs are on hand for the big announcement. Some even make sure the location makes a statement. Robert Kennedy announced his candidacy from the Senate Caucus Room, the same spot as his brother, John. With lots of fanfare and excitement, the candidate says something like, "I'm throwing my hat into the ring and running because the time has come for peace, prosperity, and security in our great country."

Once the announcement is made, the supporters all proclaim that this is good news for the country, the people, even the world. And from that moment on, every time the candidate is introduced, you hear, "Please welcome the next president of the United States!"

The Gospel of Mark is no different. Mark 1:1 begins with his announcement, "*The beginning of the gospel about Jesus Christ, the Son of God.*" Mark is telling us this is good news. The word "gospel" means "good news". And this good news is just beginning. He proclaims that Jesus is the Christ, the Son of God. Just for the record,

13

Christ is not the last name of Jesus. Christ is the Greek word for Messiah. It means the Anointed One. Messiah is the office for which Jesus is campaigning. Essentially Mark has just stood on the stage and said, "I've got good news for you! Please welcome Jesus the Messiah!"

The Jews have been looking and waiting for the Messiah to come and save them for centuries. Talk to an Orthodox Jew today and he or she will tell you they are still anticipating his arrival. By the time Jesus arrives on the scene, the Jews had been waiting for centuries. The scriptures have promised the Messiah will come from God, will deliver Israel from their enemies, and will restore the kingdom of Israel to its glory. (Isaiah 49 is a great example.) This is a very political hope.

Here is why. In the first century, the Jews had been living under foreign occupation for hundreds of years. They lost their independence in 586 BC when the Babylonians wiped out Jerusalem and took many into exile. After they were allowed to return to their homeland in 538 BC, they were still not free. They were subjects of the Medes and Persian Empires, the Greeks and the Romans. So to talk of a Messiah was to talk of freedom, deliverance, and restored glory. It was like hearing the slogans "Hope and Change" combined with "Make America Great Again." This is the context in which Mark makes his announcement. You couldn't be more political if you tried.

Not much has really changed in our own day. People are still looking for a messiah and there are plenty from which to choose. These messiah candidates promise to save the day, deliver us from our problems, destroy our enemies, and restore the glory of the nation. We pin our hopes and happiness, our significance and security on their personalities and platforms. That is one of the reasons we cannot have a civil conversation about politics in our society. We are all too busy defending our messiahs. And when our messiah loses or is exposed as false, things get ugly. The rancor and hostility displayed at such times is evidence that we have put our trust in created things (candidates, parties, government programs, etc.) rather than our Creator. False messiahs can promise all they want, but in the end they will disappoint. Yet we keep looking for the One true Messiah who can deliver. In the midst of a crowded field throughout history, Jesus is throwing His hat into the ring. Could He be the One?

He begins His campaign differently than so many we see today. There is not a lot of hype to it. His kickoff event leaves much to be desired. He does not start in the Temple in Jerusalem, nor does He go to the halls of power in Rome. He begins in the desert with a strange man baptizing people in the Jordan river. The man is John and he's not exactly the guy you want introducing you as you start your campaign.

John is not well connected, nor does he have lots of money. (Just look at his wardrobe and diet! Can you imagine a fundraiser dinner consisting of locusts and wild honey while wearing the latest fashions in camel hair?) I can't imagine John has many friends either. He is calling the nation to repentance, especially the religious leaders. He is quoting the prophet Isaiah and telling the people to get ready, the Lord is coming. Some people even begin to think John might be running for Messiah, but he made it clear that he is expecting someone else. *"After me will come one more powerful than I, the thongs of whose sandals I am not worthy to untie. I baptize you with water, but he will baptize you with the Holy Spirit."*

It might be one thing to go against the religious establishment, but John even gets sideways with the ruling class. His message gets political. Crazy mixing religion and politics, right? He calls out King Herod for marrying his brother's wife. Herod has John thrown in prison and eventually beheaded for covering this scandal in his sermons. (See Mark 6:14–29.) Most people would consider John the Baptist to be politically naïve, inept, or even toxic.

But Jesus begins His campaign by being baptized by John. This is His kickoff event. There are no big speeches, no screaming crowds, no celebrities or confetti for that matter. Jesus gets dunked by the weird desert guy to begin His campaign. Why? Because of what baptism symbolizes. It is a break from the old and an ushering in of the new. Baptism declares that the old way is dead and buried and the new way has come. For an individual baptized, it is the beginning of a new life, a new creation. It is a fresh start.

The baptism of Jesus is the beginning of the new creation, what Jesus will call the kingdom of God. There are echoes here of Genesis 1:2 before God begins to create. *"Now the earth was formless and empty, darkness was over the surface of the deep, and the Spirit of God was hovering over the waters."* This was the condition of the world before God began to call order out of chaos. As Jesus comes up out of the water, we see the Spirit of God descend upon Him. This is a new beginning for the world. This candidate is offering hope and change in a world of brokenness and chaos. But how do we know this is what Jesus means as He begins His campaign? And where does He get that kind of authority?

Mark tells us that Jesus picks up an endorsement. *"As Jesus was coming up out of the water He saw heaven being torn open and the Spirit descending on Him like a dove. And a voice came from heaven: 'You are my Son, whom I love; with you I am well pleased.'"* What would a candidate do for an endorsement like that these days!

Endorsements always come with a cost. Call me cynical, but somebody somewhere is expecting a payoff from their endorsement or large donation. That's how politics work. Even the idealist ends up compromised because of what it takes to win a nomination or election. How much of their ideals and soul remain intact after the election is anybody's guess. There are all kinds of temptations to be faced in office. Remaining true to your convictions requires someone who has been tested and found true. What would Jesus end up doing because of this endorsement?

His hat is in the ring. Now it is time to be vetted.

Discussion Questions:

1. Does it bother you to see the gospel in a political manner? Is this good news or fake news? How so?
2. Have people put their trust in created things like politicians and parties for hope and happiness, significance and security? What is the outcome of doing such a thing?

3. Have you ever placed your trust in a politician or political party? What happened?
4. What does baptism mean? What does it mean for Jesus as He starts His campaign?
5. What have you seen candidates do as a result of an endorsement or support?
6. What do you think Jesus will do as a result of His endorsement?

VETTED

---•---

Mark 1:12–13, Matthew 4:1–11

If I were two-faced, would I be wearing this one?
—Abraham Lincoln

Every candidate is examined and scrutinized to see who they are, what they stand for, what issues may present problems for them, and what skeletons they have in their past. Some candidates get a pass from the press. Others never make it past an announcement. It is not uncommon to be excited about a candidate at first, and then watch them fade away as they are sized up and checked out fairly or unfairly. The sooner the vetting takes place, the better for everyone involved.

Immediately after receiving His heavenly endorsement, Jesus hits the campaign trail and is tested. His first stop on the campaign trail is very unusual. He is led into the wilderness for forty days with no food or water. There He is tempted by Satan. You can see the temptations in detail in Matthew's Gospel, chapter 4:1–11. Mark doesn't include them, but they are worth examining briefly because they are still temptations that must be faced by any candidate today.

Satan tempts Jesus, *"If you are the Son of God, tell these stones to turn into bread."* In other words, use your power and position to satisfy your desires and needs. This temptation is always present for those who have power and position. Many politicians decide to run for office because they see power and position as an opportunity instead of a temptation. How many messiahs have left office richer and fatter than when they went into "public service"? How many of their actions in office turned stones into bread for themselves and those closest to them while neglecting their duty?

Jesus has none of it, even after going without food for forty days! He responds by quoting Scripture and relying on God to provide. *"It is written: Man does not live on bread alone, but on every word that comes from the mouth of God."*

The next temptation Jesus faces is self-promotion and justification. Satan has Him stand on the highest part of the temple. *"If you are the Son of God, throw yourself down. For it is written: He will command his angels concerning you, and they will lift you up in their hands, so that you will not strike your foot against a stone."* Do a miracle! Make a name for yourself! Grab the headlines! If God has endorsed you, He won't let anything bad happen to you. Prove that God is on your side.

In case you haven't figured it out by now, you can make the Bible say just about anything to justify yourself or your position. People on both sides of the aisle have done this to justify things like slavery, abortion, sexual immorality, violence, racism, envy, theft, and many other evils. Satan quotes Psalm 91:11–12 to tempt Jesus to justify Himself.

But again Jesus doesn't bite. Proof-texting a passage of Scripture doesn't prove anything. It must be read contextually and completely. Isolated verses can be used to support just about anything. Issues should be examined based on the entirety of Scripture. And so Jesus responds, *"It is **also** (bold mine) written: Do not put the Lord your God to the test."* Jesus relies on the whole Word of God, not bits and pieces to suit His own agenda.

His third temptation is to take a shortcut. Satan offers Jesus all the kingdoms of the world and their glory if Jesus would just bow down and worship him. The Greek implies that Jesus needs to bow down just once. Just worship one time and you get the glory without the sacrifice. Just relax your principles for a minute, compromise a little bit, and the world is yours.

Who doesn't want the shortcut? Who wouldn't go after the glory and avoid the sacrifice, the humiliation of standing alone, the hard work of going against the "conventional wisdom"? Shortcuts never take you where they promise. Compromise your convictions a little one time and it is much harder to stand your ground the next. I wonder what candidates have bowed down to in order to get an endorsement, a donation, a committee chair, a nomination. If this world is ever going to be set right, we will need a candidate who will not bow down or take shortcuts.

Jesus knows that to worship something means you would have to serve it. So He again goes to Scripture to stand firm, *"Away from me, Satan! For it is written: Worship the Lord your God and serve him only."* What we worship we will serve. It is the root of the problems in this world. We look to created things rather than the Creator. We would rather serve donkeys and elephants, thinking they hold the solutions to issues we face, rather than humbling ourselves before God and putting our trust in Him. Again, it is simply ole-fashioned idolatry. See Romans 1:21–32 for an ancient cultural analysis that remains quite contemporary.

Jesus begins His candidacy with a forty-day fasting retreat in the desert. He does so because He knows these temptations are real for any candidate. Jesus faces them head on and overcomes them. While He wins this first bout with temptation, it would not be the last time He encounters it. We will see Jesus feed thousands with bread and perform all kinds of show stopping miracles. Yet after these, He often goes off alone to pray or asks people to keep the miracle quiet. Temptation, even for Jesus, is not a one-time thing. Yet He overcomes it. Can we say that about other candidates?

How many politicians, I wonder, would run for office today if a forty-day fast in the wilderness was required upon announcing their candidacy? Are there a few politicians you'd like to see in the desert without food or water for forty days?

Discussion Questions:

1. How would you vet a candidate?
2. What temptations do you think candidates face? How would you recommend they fight them?
3. How do you resist temptation to use power and position for personal gain?
4. What issues do people use Scripture to justify their position? Do they use all of the Scripture or just a few proof texts?
5. What short cuts or compromises have you seen candidates take to get elected? When have you been tempted to take a short cut or compromise principles to get ahead?

The Stump Speech

---•---

Mark 1:14–43

It usually takes me more than three weeks to
prepare a good impromptu speech.

—Mark Twain

And so the campaign gets under way. Every candidate needs a
good stump speech stating what they are about and what they are
going to do. They need to cast a vision in a short and concise manner. Candidates give that speech over and over in as many places as
they can. Jesus begins doing exactly that in Galilee. *"The time has
come,"* He said. *"The kingdom of God is near. Repent and believe the
good news!"*

Try to put yourself in the place of a first-century Jew who comes
to a rally to hear Jesus give His stump speech. You are standing among
people who are longing to be free and independent, waiting for God
to send the Messiah to deliver Israel from her enemies. You hear Jesus
say, *"The time has come. The kingdom of God is near. Repent and believe
the good news."* You hear a politically explosive claim! Change is in
the air! Freedom! Jesus is not ignorant of the current political context. He knows exactly what He is saying and how it will be received.

We spiritualize everything Jesus said. We hear the words of Jesus
and think He spoke with a far-off look in His eyes and walked around
in a mystical daze. We hear Him say "kingdom of God" and think
of a heavenly state, the ways things ought to be. Certainly we don't

expect His words to imply that the Kingdom of God would have a direct impact on our worldly concerns. After all, isn't the Kingdom of God the place good people go after they die? Surely we don't expect the Kingdom of God in the here and now, do we?

But what if the Kingdom of God is actually near? What if it shows up? What is it and what would it look like? The Kingdom of God is wherever and whenever God's rule and reign are present. While humanity has been in rebellion against His rule and reign since Genesis 3, God has been breaking into history to demonstrate He is the ruler of heaven and earth. From the Tower of Babel in Genesis 11, to Pharaoh in Exodus, to Nebuchadnezzar in Daniel 4, to Caesar in the New Testament, God shows up and demonstrates that He is Lord of heaven and earth. God also reveals through the Psalms and the prophets that He is going to restore His rule and reign throughout all the earth through a Chosen One, an Anointed One—the Messiah. This has to have political ramifications, don't you think?

Today, people believe that combining spiritual and earthly power is Old Testament thinking and New Testament thinking separates spiritual and earthly powers. Yet, Jesus teaches us to pray, *"Thy kingdom come, Thy will be done **on earth** as it is in heaven."* What do you think He means by that? He says in Matthew 5:17, *"Do not think that I have come to abolish the Law or the Prophets; I have not come to abolish them, but to fulfill them."* Jesus knows the political ramifications and the hopes a Messiah represents. He plans to fulfill them all.

The earliest creed of the church, "Jesus is Lord," is in direct contradiction to the emperor worship throughout the Roman Empire that declared, "Caesar is Lord." Clearly, the first-century Christians understood the direct confrontation to the political order that Jesus represented and they paid for it with their lives. Many around the world today still do.

In his book, *How God Became King*, N. T. Wright says, "It doesn't take a PhD in political philosophy to know what the world's powers will do to those who act and speak to bring about God's kingdom. As well as all the other elements in the gospel story, we must recognize this for what it is, a telling of the story of Jesus as the clash between the kingdom of God and the kingdoms of the world" (p. 138).

With all of this in the background, Jesus goes around Galilee giving His stump speech. He begins to gather an inner circle, the disciples. He demonstrates what the Kingdom of God looks like as He heals people and drives out demons. His campaign stops generally happen in synagogues and people pack the places to hear Him. The crowds are *"amazed at His teaching, because He taught them as one who had authority, not as teachers of the law."* Jesus has gravitas. The people see that His authority doesn't come from quoting someone else or from some other person or institution. He speaks plainly and forthrightly. He doesn't do the political dance on issues. He doesn't speak and not say anything—as other candidates are so adept at doing. He is not politically correct as we shall see shortly. Jesus calls it like it is and like today, that amazes people.

He gives people a taste of the Kingdom of God and why they should vote for Him. News spreads quickly about Him all over the region and an entire town gathered at His door. He continues to heal people who have various diseases and drive out demons, but *"would not let the demons speak because they knew who He was."* Does it make you wonder what they know about Jesus that He doesn't want out in the open? Is there a scandal brewing?

Hardly. They know Jesus is the Holy One of God and is bringing in the Kingdom of God. Jesus knows the sooner people begin to speak of Him as the Messiah, the sooner He will attract the attention of the religious and political establishment and their opposition. He is trying to get the word out and move fast before that opposition arrives. And so while His poll numbers are growing and everyone is coming to Him, He tells His campaign staff it is time to hit the road. They begin traveling to other towns to give His stump speech.

Jesus continues to preach and heal; attracting so many people that He is unable to enter a town openly. He is so popular that He is forced to stay in what Mark calls "lonely places." Yet even in the middle of nowhere, people come to him from everywhere. His rallies are standing room only. Things are going great. So great that those in positions of power become a bit concerned. They begin to pay closer attention to this outsider.

Discussion Questions:

1. What comes to mind when you hear "Kingdom of God"?
2. How would you explain the Kingdom of God to someone?
3. What would the rule and reign of God look like in today's world? In your life? What would change?
4. What do you think Jesus meant when He taught people to pray, "May Your kingdom come, may Your will be done on earth as it is in heaven"?
5. Is the creed, "Jesus is Lord" a political statement today? If so, how? If not, why not?
6. How do the actions of Jesus help explain what the Kingdom of God looks like on earth as it is in heaven?

OPPOSITION

Mark 2:1–8:26

Voter: "I wouldn't vote for you, if you were St. Peter himself!"
Candidate: "If I were St. Peter, you wouldn't be in my district!"

With popularity comes contempt. Jesus now has the attention of the religious leaders, the establishment. Outsiders are never welcomed into existing power structures. They are a threat and must be taken down, exposed, and branded as unqualified pretenders. The religious leaders want to check out this new upstart so they go to His rally in Capernaum. And it is a circus. The place is packed. So many people are jammed in that there is no room even outside. Four guys go so far as to tear open the roof and lower a paralytic through the ceiling in hopes Jesus would heal him.

And then it happens, in front of God and everyone. Jesus says something politically incorrect. He looks at this man lying paralyzed in front of Him and says, *"Son, your sins are forgiven."* The teachers of the law immediately start tweeting, "Who does this guy think he is? He's blaspheming!" The fact checkers report in, "Only God can forgive sins." Jesus has just claimed the power of God for Himself. People are thinking, "Does this guy think He is God?" I'm sure Jesus is not the only candidate to think he was God, but actually acting on it is no way to run a campaign. This is the first crisis of the campaign. How is Jesus going to spin this?

He doesn't. He answers directly. He is never afraid of tough questions and is always willing to engage in a discussion of the issues. Jesus responds with a question of His own. *"Which is easier: to say to the paralytic, 'Your sins are forgiven,' or to say, 'Get up, take your mat and walk?"*

I don't know about you but I'd say option A is easier. How would anyone know if the man's sins were not forgiven? You can't prove it one way or the other. A regular politician would go with the unverifiable statement. It is much safer. Actually a regular candidate would never have said anything remotely like what Jesus says to this man. But then Jesus has raised the stakes on Himself by posing the second option, getting up and walking, which can be verified.

It appears to be a rookie mistake. It is bad enough to say "Your sins are forgiven," but whether it is true or not could be debated until Elijah returned. It would have blown over. But now Jesus has given the opposition all they need to discredit Him. If this man doesn't get up and walk out of there with his mat under his arm, Jesus is a fraud. He has no authority to say what He said. The religious leaders will run Him out of town.

However, the opposition never gets a chance to answer the question as to which is easier. Jesus continues, *"But that you may know that the Son of Man has authority on earth to forgive sins...."* And then looking at the paralytic He said, *"I tell you get up, take your mat and go home."* And the man does! Everyone sees it. And the place goes nuts! The people have never seen anything like it. They all praise God and are amazed at Jesus' power and authority.

Well, not all. When you are the authority and in power, you don't praise God for someone else's authority or power. Especially when their power and authority doesn't come from you. You are not amazed. You are threatened. And so the Pharisees and religious leaders begin to keep a close eye on Jesus looking for ways to discredit Him.

They begin asking questions like, *"Why does He eat with tax collectors and sinners?"* They are not Hollywood A-listers, not the power brokers in Jerusalem, not the cultural elite. They are the deplorables.

They ask why His disciples don't fast like everyone else. In other words, Jesus isn't playing by their rules. He is not running a conventional campaign. He is an outsider. All of these questions are in the air, being debated by the know-it-alls of the day. It creates a cloud of suspicion around the campaign.

And then scandal hits! His disciples are charged with breaking the law. They are picking grain on the Sabbath. It's Graingate! The religious leaders work very hard to make sure no one does any work on the Sabbath. Walking more than a short distance is forbidden, much less walking through a grain field and snacking on the grain. They are caught in the act by the Pharisees. Which makes me wonder: if it is against the law to be walking more than a short distance on the Sabbath, how is it that the Pharisees could be in the grain field to see what the disciples are doing and then immediately call Jesus out on it?

Jesus holds a press conference and answers the question. He offers a response from the scriptures basically saying they miss the whole point of the Sabbath and then drops a bombshell on them with His closing remark, *"So the Son of Man is Lord even of the Sabbath."*

Let's pause for a moment and examine what Jesus has just said. By claiming to be Lord of the Sabbath, He is saying that He is the only one who can rightly determine what the purpose of the Sabbath is and how to properly keep it. All of their man-made laws are meaningless. He has just upended hundreds of years of tradition.

But wait, there's more! This is the second time Jesus uses this title, Son of Man, to refer to Himself. (The first time was when He healed the paralytic.) This title is used eighty-one times in the four Gospels and never used by anyone but Jesus. It comes from Daniel 7:13–14, *"In my vision at night I looked and there before me was one like a son of man, coming with the clouds of heaven. He approached the Ancient of Days and was led into his presence. He was given authority, glory, and sovereign power; all peoples, nations and men of every language worshipped Him. His dominion is an everlasting dominion that will not pass away and His kingdom is one that will never be destroyed."*

Is Jesus trying to tell us something about Himself with this title? Hmmm? And do you think the "experts" in the law missed what He was saying?

After "Graingate," Jesus is at another rally in a synagogue. The establishment is there watching to see if they can accuse Jesus. Of what, even they don't know. They are not interested in hearing anything He has to say. They are looking for a way to discredit Him. They see a man with a shriveled hand in the crowd and so they are hoping Jesus will heal the man. Not because they care for the man, but because it is the Sabbath and healing would be doing work. Working on the Sabbath is against the law, thus Jesus becomes a lawbreaker. Campaign over.

The Pharisees are watching Jesus closely and can't believe their eyes when Jesus asks the man with the shriveled hand to stand up. This is it! They think they've got Him! Stop for a second. Can you imagine people so twisted that they hope for a man's shriveled hand to be healed so they can accuse the healer of breaking the law? What would cause that in people? Simple: power and position. British historian Lord John Acton famously said, "Power tends to corrupt. And absolute power corrupts absolutely." When power and position are threatened, things get ugly.

Jesus has the man stand up in front of everyone and then asks, *"Which is lawful on the Sabbath: to do good or to do evil, to save life or to kill?" But they remained silent.* Nothing but crickets. Why don't they answer? To answer they would have to say, "to do good, to save life." It is absurd to say it is lawful to do evil or to kill on the Sabbath. But to do good requires effort. To save life would probably require extraordinary measures, breaking the man-made laws of the Sabbath. To answer Jesus would be to admit that they are wrong about the Sabbath and their interpretation of the Law, and that Jesus is right. Have you ever seen people admit they are wrong in a campaign? Me neither. So they remain silent.

"Jesus looked around at them in anger, and deeply distressed at their stubborn hearts, said to the man, 'Stretch out your hand.' He stretched it out and it was completely restored." Do you notice that the only people

Jesus seems to be angry with are the people with stubborn hearts? He is around all kinds of "sinners and tax collectors," yet He willingly welcomes them. But time and again, the only ones who grate His cheese are the ones hanging on to their pride and position. In the face of a wonderful miracle, the Pharisees begin to plot with the Herodians how they might kill Jesus. Yes, you read that right, they want to kill Jesus for healing a guy.

Let's take a moment and see who exactly is the opposition. Who are the Pharisees and the Herodians and why do they want to team up and kill Jesus?

The Pharisees are part of the religious establishment. (We will see another part, the Sadducees, later when we get to Jerusalem.) They are the keepers of the Law of God and the traditions of the Hebrew faith. They went to the right schools, have the right pedigree, etc. They have their status and power through their interpretation of the Law of God. They get to say what is correct and incorrect according to God in the lives of the people. They have been checking Jesus out to see what He is teaching and practicing. If Jesus is going to teach and practice what will expand their kingdom and power, fine. But He is a threat because He isn't playing by their rules. He doesn't have the right background and pedigree. And He is leading in the polls. Crowds are following Him everywhere. Jesus threatens to overturn their establishment, their hold on power and they can't have that.

The Herodians are the political class that wants to see a member of Herod's family on the throne of Judea as the king of the Jews. They are not very religious as they beheaded John the Baptist as a dinner party gift. They support Roman occupation because the Romans give them their power and position. The Herod family is not Jewish so anytime someone begins to campaign as the Messiah, the king of the Jews, they get a bit sideways. Think King Herod and Christmas. (Herod being the monster that ordered all the male children under two to be slaughtered in Bethlehem after the wise men came through town looking for *"the one who has been born king of the Jews."* See Matthew 2:1–18. That Herod is now dead and his sons split up the kingdom and each have their own throne.) With Jesus running an open campaign for the office of Messiah, He is a direct political threat to the Herodians. The conflict they have with Jesus is pretty obvious.

What is fascinating about the Pharisees and the Herodians teaming up is that they don't like each other. It would be like the NRA and PETA teaming up. The Pharisees see the family of Herod as imposters on the throne of David. They are not descendants of King David and have no claim to be on the throne. They are there because Rome has put them in power. One more reason to hate Rome. Politics has made stranger bedfellows, I suppose. Jesus is a threat to the power and position of both. In their minds, He must be stopped.

Jesus is a threat because His kingdom is not their kingdom. Is that any different today? Many people, even politicians, will claim Jesus so long as He goes along with their position, answers prayers according to their desires, or advances their cause. It would be good right now to pause and answer this question: Do you pray for His kingdom to come or yours?

Yet, even in spite of the opposition, Jesus continues to climb in the polls through the primaries. People are coming to Him from all over. They crowd Him, pushing and shoving just to touch Him, because He is healing so many. He has picked His team of campaign managers and assistants, the disciples. He continues traveling, preaching about the Kingdom of God, giving signs that it is near, even breaking into existence among them. He teaches in parables that are very retweetable, heals the sick, makes the blind see, and the lame walk. He brings a dead girl back to life, walks on water, and feeds five thousand with a bag lunch. Candidates promise miracles if they are elected; Jesus is actually delivering. No wonder His poll numbers are through the roof.

Every time Jesus casts out demons, they acknowledge that He is the Son of God. And when He calms a storm in front of His disciples, they ask each other, *"Who is this? Even the wind and the waves obey Him."* That is the question, isn't it? Who is this Jesus? How can He do all these incredible things?

The establishment has an answer. They go on every talk show they can, following Jesus around, accusing Him of being demon-possessed. They say He gets His power from the prince of demons. Looks like demonizing your political opponent is not a new trick at all! When all you can do is challenge your opponent on washing their hands incorrectly before they eat, name calling becomes the most plausible strategy. *"He's out of His mind!" "He's possessed by Beelzebub!"* Today, we would just invoke the names of Hitler and Stalin.

But it doesn't slow down the campaign. Mark 7:37 says, *"People were overwhelmed with amazement. 'He has done everything well,' they said. 'He even makes the deaf hear and the mute speak.'"* As the primaries come to a close and we head into the convention, we have to ask: Who is this Jesus? Whose kingdom are you praying will come? What kind of Messiah are you looking for? Jesus is campaigning and you are going to have to vote.

Discussion Questions:

1. Who can you think of that has run for office as an outsider? How were they treated?
2. Jesus eats with tax collectors and sinners. Is this smart campaigning? Why does it bother the elites?
3. What is Jesus trying to tell us by using the title, "the Son of Man"? Do you think the experts of the law understood what He was saying?
4. What kind of political language is used in Daniel 7:13–14?
5. Is Lord John Acton right that "power tends to corrupt and absolute power corrupts absolutely."? Can you think of any examples where power didn't corrupt?
6. Who is it that Jesus is angry and distressed by: sinners or stubborn people? Is it still true today? Which are you?
7. Why is Jesus a threat to the establishment?
8. What kind of Messiah are you looking for?

THE CONVENTION

---•---

Mark 8:27–9:13

Nonviolence is the answer to the crucial political and moral
questions of our time; the need for man to overcome oppression
and violence without resorting to oppression and violence.
Man must evolve for all human conflict a method
which rejects revenge, aggression, and retaliation.
The foundation of such a method is love.

—Martin Luther King Jr.
accepting the Nobel Peace Prize, 1964

THE NOMINATION

Mark 8:27–29

After four years at the United Nations, I sometimes yearn
for the peace and tranquility of a political convention.
—Adlai E. Stevenson

Political conventions are quite the show. These days everything is
scripted beforehand, even who will get the nomination. Usually parties hold their conventions in cities where they have lots of support.
There is nothing like home-field advantage. Sometimes parties will
go to places where they are hoping to swing a state in their direction.

For Jesus the convention is, of all places, in Caesarea Philippi.
Odd choice for a Jewish Messiah. This was a pagan town dedicated
to the worship of the Greek god Pan. The people built shrines to the
fertility god in the cliffs above the city. The people believed the gods
would go to and from the underworld through a cave at the bottom
of the cliff and would perform crude sexual acts there in worship.
The cave was thought to be a gate to the underworld. The people
living in Jesus' time thought this city was at the entrance of Hades.
That means Jesus was holding his political convention at the gates of
hell. Interesting choice.

As they approach Caesarea Philippi, Jesus takes a straw poll.
"On the way, He asked them, 'Who do people say I am?'" That is the
question that keeps popping up in this campaign. Who is Jesus?

And surprisingly, the answers are not much different today than what He gets. *"They replied, 'Some say John the Baptist, others say Elijah, and still others one of the prophets.'"* Today people say Jesus was a prophet, a good teacher, a moral example, a myth or legend, even one of the ways to God. These are all fine answers because they keep our options open. We can like Jesus without having to commit to Him. Once you nominate a candidate you're stuck with him or her, for better or for worse.

I spoke with a lady after a funeral once who would have been one of those in the straw poll who said Jesus was a good teacher, a moral example, "one who pointed us to the mysteries beyond" were her exact words. But the Messiah, the Son of God? Nope, that is too exclusive. After all, it's important to have options.

I shared with her what C. S. Lewis so famously said about the question, "Who is Jesus?" He said you basically have three options with Jesus. He is either a liar who claimed to be something He wasn't (the Messiah, the Son of God), a lunatic on the level of a poached egg for making the claims He made, or He was who He said He was— Lord. Liar, lunatic, or Lord—those are your options. Just a good teacher, a moral example, or one of the prophets is illogical.

But Jesus isn't so much concerned about the polls and what other people think of Him as much as He is interested in who you think He is. He asks his disciples, *"But what about you? Who do you say I am?"* He is looking for the nomination. Remember this is the question Mark continually brings forward in his gospel, "Who is Jesus?" And every one of us has to answer it. Here is Jesus, asking for the nomination.

"But what about you? Who do you say that I am?" Peter answered, "You are the Christ."

Discussion Questions:

1. Have you ever been to a political convention? What was it like?

2. What is Jesus saying by holding His convention at the gates of hell? How do you think the opposition would spin it?
3. Do you agree with C. S. Lewis that Jesus has to be either a liar, a lunatic, or Lord? Is there another option?
4. Who do you say Jesus is?

THE PLATFORM

---◆·◆---

Mark 8:30–9:1

We will have so much winning if I get elected
that you may get bored with winning.

—Donald Trump

Acceptance speeches are the culmination of a convention. They are huge media events as people all over the country tune in to hear what the candidate is going to do if elected. Tons of work goes into making sure everything is perfect. One slip up and the campaign may never recover. The 1972 Democratic Convention in Miami is a good example. Disgruntled delegates nominated, among others, Archie Bunker and Mao Tse-tung to the ticket. The circus caused McGovern's acceptance speech to be delayed until 3:00 AM where it is remembered as "prime time in Guam." Needless to say, Nixon won the election of '72.

Now that Jesus has the nomination, He gives his acceptance speech and lays out His platform. "Here is what I am going to do as the Messiah." Except this speech heads south before it even begins. As soon as Jesus gets the nomination from Peter, He immediately warns them not to tell anyone about Him. That is going to make publicity and press conferences difficult.

But it gets worst. *"He then began to teach them that the Son of Man must suffer many things and be rejected by the elders, chief*

38

priests, and teachers of the law, and that He must be killed and after three days rise again." Can you imagine? Jesus steps to the microphone after receiving the nomination and announces His platform, "Hey guys, I am going to lose!" Strike up the band and drop the balloons.

Peter, the campaign manager, immediately goes into damage control mode. He pulls Jesus aside and lays into Him. "That is not a winning strategy! Nobody wants a Messiah with a death wish!" And Peter begins to lay out a different strategy for victory.

What kind of strategy would you lay out for the Messiah? I'm sure you have thought, "If my candidate would just say this…or do that…they would win in a landslide." Cause after all, that's the point of an election—winning! You can't win if you're dead.

Let me stop you right here and tell you something about Jesus. He does not listen to political advisors. He knows where their wisdom comes from. In the harshest terms possible, He rebukes Peter. *"Get behind me Satan! You do not have in mind the things of God, but the things of men."*

And without missing a beat, He doubles down on His "losing" platform and declares what party membership looks like. *"If anyone would come after me, he must deny himself, take up his cross and follow me. For whoever wants to save his life will lose it, but whoever loses his life for me and for the gospel will save it. What good is it for a man to gain the whole world and forfeit his soul? Or what can a man give in exchange for his soul?"*

This speech goes against all conventional wisdom. Not only is Jesus saying He is going to lose, but He is calling everyone who joins His party to lose as well. This is nuts. You can just see the convention hall emptying out.

But what does Jesus mean by having in mind the things of men and losing my life for Him?

To have in mind the things of men is to win power, status, and build a kingdom or legacy for myself. It is to do great things for the world to see. And when the world sees my greatness, they will build monuments to me. I will have gained the whole world. That is the desire of every man and woman from Pharaoh to Nebuchadnezzar to Caesar to Emperors to Dictators and every other false messiah to come along promising hope and change or to make a nation great again.

To lose myself for Him means I surrender all of that and pursue His kingdom. I deny myself the power, status, legacy, fame, and everything else this world offers so that Jesus receives the glory, honor, and praise of all the Earth. I surrender my kingdom and seek His kingdom to come on Earth as it is in heaven. Doing this may very well cost you your life because false messiahs don't like the competition. His kingdom threatens their kingdoms. Does His kingdom threaten yours?

Back in the convention hall this speech is not playing well. Peter and the disciples have to be panicking. Maybe all the criticism from the establishment is right. Maybe Jesus is off His rocker. This is embarrassing. Maybe we need to find a new candidate.

Jesus finishes His speech, *"If anyone is ashamed of me and my words in this adulterous and sinful generation, the Son of Man will be ashamed of him when He comes in His Father's glory and with the holy angels. I tell you the truth, some who are standing here will not taste death before they see the kingdom of God come with power."*

As Jesus steps away from the podium, the commentators analyzing the speech begin to rip it apart. "He talks about losing and death, but then about coming in His Father's glory and seeing the Kingdom of God with power. How is that supposed to happen if you lose?"

"He seems to be all over the place with grand pronouncements but offering no specifics."

"This is what happens when you don't use a Teleprompter."

"Another demonstration that Jesus is unfit to lead."

"No matter what, this convention will go down in history."

"Wait, this just in. Three close advisors of Jesus are taking Him on a mountain retreat to see if they can salvage this campaign. Stay tuned for further developments."

Discussion Questions:

1. What kind of strategy/platform would you lay out for the Messiah?
2. What is Jesus' platform?
3. How would you rate His acceptance speech?
4. What does Jesus say party membership looks like?
5. Would you join His party? What would you have to lose to join? What would you gain?

THE ENDORSEMENT

Mark 9:2–8

Politics is supposed to be the second oldest profession. I have come to realize that it bears a very close resemblance to the first.

—Ronald Reagan

When campaigns stagnate, an endorsement can breathe life back into it. Momentum can shift, gaffes can be forgotten, blunders forgiven. In 1960, JFK worked hard to get Democrat and liberal icon Eleanor Roosevelt to switch her endorsement from Adlai Stevenson. She made a commercial for Kennedy encouraging people to study his record and vote for him. Her endorsement helped give Kennedy standing among social liberals of the day and swing the party's nomination in his direction.

Candidates do all kinds of things to get endorsements. If you can get the right people representing the right causes to give you the thumbs up, you can clean up. But what do you have to give up to get the endorsement? There are all kinds of backroom deals and promises made. Seats of power, political appointments, presidential pardons, and all kinds of other favors are traded in exchange for an endorsement. Candidates will even give up who they are and what they believe in, if necessary. Sure they will continue to say whatever they need to, but when it comes time to act, the mask comes off and everyone sees who they really are.

Jesus takes his three closest disciples up a mountain. Peter, James, and John are probably trying to wrap their heads around what happened at the convention. A few days in the mountain air might give them some clarity on their situation and how to move forward. Perhaps they are thinking this is going to be a strategic planning retreat. But Jesus has something else in mind.

There on the top of the mountain, Jesus is transfigured before them. *"His clothes became dazzling white, whiter than anyone could bleach them."* The disciples see exactly what Jesus said some would see at the end of His acceptance speech: the Kingdom of God come with power! They see Jesus for who He really is—in His glory! His transfiguration is a change on the outside that reveals who He really is on the inside. False messiahs masquerade. They change their outside to hide their inward reality. Here, Jesus changes His outside to reveal His inner reality.

But that's not all. Standing next to Jesus in His glory and power are Moses and Elijah. They are talking with Jesus. What are they talking about? Perhaps they are going to endorse Jesus. This would be huge! Moses and Elijah are the two biggest names in Israel. Moses represents the Law and the things that need to be conserved. Elijah represents the prophets who spoke of reform and the way things ought to be. This is exactly the boost the campaign needs to solidify the left and right. So Peter says, "It is good that we are here. Let us put up three podiums and call a press conference."

As Peter starts looking for his tool box, something else happens. *"Then a cloud appeared and enveloped them, and a voice came from the cloud: 'This is my Son, whom I love. Listen to Him!'"*

Is there anyone's endorsement that carries more weight than that of God? Whose voice are you listening to? Whose endorsement would sway your vote? A celebrity? A politician? A friend? Can you imagine Washington and Lincoln showing up to endorse a candidate today? Jesus doesn't need any of those endorsements. He gets the only endorsement that matters.

"Suddenly, when they looked around, they no longer saw anyone with them except Jesus." When the smoke clears, only Jesus is there. Moses and Elijah are gone because Jesus doesn't need the endorse-

ment of the Law or the Prophets. If you are clinging to what was or advocating for what should be, you will miss Jesus standing right in the present fulfilling both. He is the only candidate that can.

Discussion Questions:

1. Whose endorsement would sway your vote?
2. Do candidates hide who they really are? Why or why not?
3. To whom would you be willing to reveal your inward reality? From whom do you hide it?
4. Why is Jesus the only candidate that can fulfill both the Law and the Prophets?
5. What do you think Jesus, Moses, and Elijah are talking about? (Luke 9:30–31)

THE CAMPAIGN

Mark 9:9–14:10

I am a firm believer in the people.
If given the truth, they can be depended
upon to meet any national crisis.
The great point is to bring them the real facts, and beer.

—Abraham Lincoln

THE ROOT ISSUE

Mark 9:9–10:52

Politics is the art of looking for trouble, finding it everywhere, diagnosing it incorrectly, and applying the wrong remedies.
—Groucho Marx

Coming down the mountain, Peter, James, and John have to be thinking, "Jesus you put on that show a few more times and this election is in the bag." But then Jesus does it again. He orders them *"not to tell anybody what they had seen until the Son of Man had risen from the dead."* This has to be frustrating to His friends. He is back on this dying thing. What does He mean rising from the dead? Does that mean not to say anything until His poll numbers go back up? They ask a question about Elijah, but He counters with a question of His own. *"Why then is it written that the Son of Man must suffer much and be rejected?"*

Why indeed? If Jesus has this power and glory in Him, why suffer? This "losing" platform He has put out there makes no political sense at all. And it is clear He is not coming off it. So why must He suffer and be rejected?

Because Jesus is addressing the root issue. He is going after the real cause of the problems we face in the world. Every political, social, economic, environmental, national, or global problem has, at its root, our sin and separation from God. The world and everyone in it is broken because of our rebellion and refusal to submit to God.

Many today are saying the problem with the world is an unequal distribution of wealth. To fix this we need to redistribute the wealth equally. That is what the government must do. Others say the problem is patriarchy. White men control positions of power and authority. To fix the problem, women and minorities must replace them and then justice will come. Others say the problem is the government is too big and corrupt. To fix the problem we must "drain the swamp." On and on it goes.

Politicians, candidates, and false messiahs all offer solutions to the issues we face. But who has ever delivered? From the war on poverty to peace in our time, their promises are unfulfilled. They diagnose a symptom but not the real sickness. They can't fix the root issue because they, too, are sick and broken by sin and separated from God.

Jesus is different and His solution is going to be different. The Son of Man has to be rejected because of the political nature of His kingdom. His rule means others won't. Our rebellion started in the Garden of Eden. We didn't want to live by the one rule God gave. We wanted to be in charge. We wanted to be King. As a result, the world is out of whack, upside down, running opposite of the way it was created to run. Instead of unity, there is discord. Instead of peace, there is war. Instead of prosperity, there is poverty. Instead of stewardship, there is selfishness. Instead of freedom, there is slavery. Instead of life, there is death.

Our rebellion against God continues to this day. We strive to set up our own kingdoms and be our own king. But the universe is not wired to work that way. Rebellion against God (the Bible calls it sin) always results in separation from God, others, and yourself. You cannot sin successfully. It always results in the disintegration of creation. It always ends in death.

In addition, God is holy. Therefore, He cannot live in the midst of sin and rebellion. Or better said, we cannot live in the midst of His holiness. Our sin in His presence would kill us. We would literally die of embarrassment and shame. God is also just and justice requires that rebellion and sin be punished. The wrong done to God must be atoned.

The Son of Man has to suffer and die because He is going to save us from the consequences of our rebellion and sin—namely death and eternal separation from God in hell—and make atonement for us. The Son of Man is going to make creation great again—the way it was intended to be from the beginning. There have been some candidates who have suffered and died serving the people. Lincoln is the foremost of them. He was killed because of his effort to save the Union. But even with such a great sacrifice, Lincoln could not solve the root issue. Others have been a servant of the people, but all of them had sin as well.

Only someone without sin can make atonement for us and save us. We need someone who can pay the penalty for sin, reverse the curse, and turn the world right side up. We need a candidate to come along and claim Isaiah's mantle when he says in 61:1–3, *"The Spirit of the Sovereign Lord is on me, because the Lord has anointed me to preach good news to the poor. He has sent me to bind up the broken hearted, to proclaim freedom for the captives and release from darkness for the prisoners, to proclaim the year of the Lord's favor and the day of vengeance of our God, to comfort all who mourn, and provide for those who grieve in Zion—to bestow on them a crown of beauty instead of ashes, the oil of gladness instead of mourning, and a garment of praise instead of a spirit of despair."*

We need THE Messiah. This is the only fix for the root issue, for all the issues.

From this point on in the campaign, this is His focus. Jesus is all about this one issue. The whole world will swirl around Him like a hurricane. He has His eyes fixed on the cross because the cross is the only fix for the world. This is exactly what the acceptance speech was all about.

The prophet Isaiah explains it this way,

> *He was despised and rejected by men,*
> *a man of sorrows, and familiar with suffering.*
> *Like one from whom men hide their faces*
> *He was despised and we esteemed Him not.*

Surely He took up our infirmities
and carried our sorrows,
yet we considered Him stricken by God,
smitten by Him and afflicted.

But He was pierced for our transgressions,
He was crushed for our iniquities;
The punishment that brought us peace was upon Him,
and by His wounds we are healed.
We all, like sheep, have gone astray,
each of us has turned to his own way;
and the LORD has laid on Him
the iniquity of us all.

He was oppressed and afflicted,
yet He did not open His mouth;
He was led like a lamb to the slaughter,
and as sheep before her shearers is silent,
so He did not open His mouth.
By oppression and judgment, he was taken away.
And who can speak of his descendants?
For He was cut off from the land of the living;
for the transgression of my people He was stricken.
He was assigned a grave with the wicked,
and with the rich in His death,
though He had done no violence,
nor was any deceit in His mouth.

Yet it was the LORD's will to crush Him and cause
Him to suffer,
and though the LORD makes His life a guilt offering,
He will see His offspring and prolong His days,
and the will of the LORD will prosper in His hand.
After the suffering of His soul,
He will see the light of life and be satisfied;

by His knowledge my righteous servant will justify
   many,
and He will bear their iniquities.

Therefore, I will give Him a portion among the great,
and He will divide the spoils among the strong,
because He poured out His life unto death,
and was numbered with the transgressors.
For He bore the sin of many,
and made intercession for the transgressors. (Isa.
   53:3–12)

Down off the mountain, the campaign is back in full swing. Jesus is casting out demons, kissing babies, restoring sight to the blind, and enduring questions from the establishment meant to trap Him. But there are a couple new wrinkles.

Jesus isn't a big tent party guy. When a rich young ruler (a very valuable demographic in any campaign) wants to join, He tells him to sell all he has and then come follow. The guy walks away and Jesus lets Him. Losing is the platform and He doesn't compromise it for anybody.

His disciples have an internal squabble about who is the greatest and which cabinet position they should have, but Jesus redefines what greatest and leadership are. He says, *"You know that those who are regarded as rulers of the Gentiles lord it over them, and their high officials exercise authority over them. Not so with you. Instead, whoever wants to become great among you must be your servant, and whoever wants to be first must be slave to all. For the Son of Man did not come to be served, but to serve, and to give His life as a ransom for many."* Jesus flips the script on power. It is not to be used to make others do your will as is often the case in this broken and rebellious world. Jesus is demonstrating what power is meant to do—serve others, even if it means sacrifice.

And it is why Jesus keeps telling His campaign staff the end game. *"We are going up to Jerusalem and the Son of Man will be betrayed to the chief priests and teachers of the law. They will condemn Him to death and will hand Him over to the Gentiles, who will mock Him and spit on Him, flog Him, and kill Him. Three days later He will rise."*

On they go to Jerusalem.

Discussion Questions:

1. What would you say is the most important issue of the day?
2. How would you solve it?
3. What is the root issue Jesus is after?
4. What does sin do? Is it simply personal or does it affect the political nature of the world?
5. Is the universe wired to work a certain way or do we just make it up as we go? Explain your answer.
6. How is Jesus going to fix the root issue? What makes Him qualified to do so?
7. How does Isaiah 53 line up with the platform Jesus lays out at the convention? Can you find all the planks in it?
8. How does His solution turn the political nature of the world on its head?

THE FINAL PUSH

Mark 11:1–26

Politician: "Have you heard my last speech?"
Voter: "I hope so!"

It is the beginning of Passover week in Jerusalem. There are thousands of pilgrims pouring into the city to celebrate the holy festival. Passover is like Thanksgiving, Christmas, and the Fourth of July all rolled into one. It commemorates the birth of the Jewish nation and their deliverance from bondage and slavery in Egypt. So you can imagine that celebrating your independence and freedom while being under Roman occupation creates a longing for the Messiah to show up, make Israel great again, and bring in the Kingdom of God. It is a political tinderbox waiting for a spark.

And Jesus lights the match. His big entrance into the city has the whole town buzzing. He comes into town riding a donkey. Now how is that provocative? You might be thinking, "See! I knew Jesus is a Democrat!" Jesus is sending a message, but that is not it. The prophet Zechariah prophesied about the Messiah showing up in Jerusalem. He wrote in Zechariah 9:9, *"Rejoice greatly, O Daughter of Zion! Shout Daughter of Jerusalem! See, your king comes to you, righteous and having salvation, gentle and riding on a donkey, on a colt, the foal of a donkey."* Jesus is saying in the midst of this explosive setting, "I am the King." And the people know it.

They give Him the red carpet treatment as His entrance into Jerusalem turns into a political rally. They throw their cloaks down and spread branches on the ground before Him. John 12:13 says they waved palm branches. Why would they do that? The last time the nation of Israel was free from foreign powers was during the Maccabees around 160 BC. During that time they minted coins with palm branches on them. Palm branches were the symbol of their freedom and independence. Waving palm branches would be like waving the Stars and Stripes down Main Street.

Going before and behind Jesus as He rides into Jerusalem, the people are shouting, *"Hosanna!"* (It means "Save!" Or "Save us!") *"Blessed is he who comes in the name of the Lord! Blessed is the coming kingdom of our father David! Hosanna in the highest!"* Don't miss the part about the coming kingdom of our father David. The people know what the Lord promised to King David a thousand years earlier in 2 Samuel 7:16. *"Your house and your kingdom will endure forever before me; your throne will be established forever."* It is clear the people believe the Lord is fulfilling that ancient promise in their sight. They are declaring Jesus to be Messiah, the King of the Jews, who will make Israel great again.

How do you think the religious and political establishment feel about this political rally, about the crowds, about Jesus and His overt claims?

The spark is lit, and now Jesus is about to throw gas on the fire. The next day as Jesus heads back to Jerusalem, He holds an impromptu press conference by a fig tree. Old Testament prophets like Nahum and Hosea use a fig tree to symbolize the nation of Israel. Jesus sees the fig tree is in leaf and goes to find out if it has any fruit. He discovers the tree is all leaf and no fruit—all talk and no results. *"May no one eat fruit from you again."* Within twenty-four hours, the tree has withered. It is a warning to the establishment. Jesus judges the tree for not delivering what its leaf promises. And then He heads for the Temple, the epicenter of life, identity, and power in Israel.

Jesus gets to the Temple and cleans it out. He drives out the special interest groups buying and selling. He overturns the tables of the money changers. It is chaos. People are running to get out of His way. Others are scurrying to collect their belongings scattered all over the place. Jesus won't let people carry merchandise through the Temple courts. He is judging the corruption that has overtaken the Temple as He calls out, *"Is it not written: 'My house will be a house of prayer for all nations'? But you have made it 'a den of robbers.'"*

If you are part of the establishment making money and gaining power by corrupt means, what will you do to the person who calls you out on it? You would have to get rid of him. That is exactly what the chief priests and the teachers of the law want to do. But they can't because the crowd is with Jesus. So they confront Jesus and ask Him where He gets His authority to do these things.

Let the debates begin!

Discussion Questions:

1. How is riding a donkey into Jerusalem provocative?
2. How do you think the religious and political establishment feel about Jesus' entrance?
3. Why would Jesus curse a fig tree? What did it ever do to deserve that? How is that a warning or judgment? For whom?
4. Is Jesus picking a fight in the Temple? Do you think dialog would have been a better way to go?
5. What happens when an outsider calls out the corruption of the establishment?

THE DEBATES

Mark 11:27–12:40

If you ever injected truth into politics, you'd have no politics.
—Will Rogers

The first televised presidential debate was between Kennedy and Nixon. It goes down in history, not necessarily because it was the first one on TV, but because many think it changed the outcome of the election. TV made style as important (some would argue more important) than substance. During the debate, Nixon looked flustered and sweaty while Kennedy looked calm and handsome. It is interesting that those who listened to the debate on radio said Nixon won. But those who watched it on TV said Kennedy walked away with it.

I don't know if anyone watches a presidential debate to actually learn anything about the issues. They are mostly about "gotcha" moments. Like when Reagan said in 1984 running against Mondale that he would not make age an issue in the campaign. (Reagan was seventy-three running for reelection.) "I am not going to exploit, for political purposes, my opponent's youth and inexperience." Even Mondale laughed, and lost. People watch the debates to see those moments just like they watch NASCAR to see the cars wreck.

But people do watch them. And whether it is substance vs. style or who gets in the best one-liners, the debates matter because they reveal something more about the candidate than we get in a stump

56

speech, an advertisement, or a sit down interview. We get to see how they handle conflict under pressure. One slip up and it could be all over.

After His rally riding into Jerusalem and turning the Temple on its ear, Jesus walks right into the debates. More accurately, the debates walk right into Jesus. The religious establishment begins with this question, *"By what authority are you doing these things?" "And who gave you authority to do this?"* Notice they don't challenge what He did or refute His charges of corruption. They can't. They challenge His authority essentially saying, "You are not qualified to tell us anything."

Jesus welcomes their question and is willing to answer it, but first He wants to see if they are going to deal honestly with Him. He wants to make sure it is a level playing field and that the game isn't rigged. So He answered, *"I will ask you one question. Answer me and I will tell you by what authority I am doing these things. John's baptism— was it from heaven or from men? Tell me!"* The establishment and elites huddle up and try to come up with an answer. Dr. John Rankin explains their options in his book, *Jesus in the Face of His Enemies*:

Option A: They could admit the truth that it was from heaven. However, they realize, *"If we say 'From heaven,' He will ask, 'Then why didn't you believe him?'"* The establishment cannot admit to the truth because they will not submit to the truth.

Option B: Market a lie and say it was the people's imagination or wishful thinking that John had authority from heaven. *"But if we say, 'From men'... (They feared the people, for everyone held that John really was a prophet.)"* They don't want the crowd to turn against them so they come up with option C.

Option C: Feign ignorance. They go with option C and answer Jesus with, *"We don't know."*

Dr. Rankin writes, "The 'I don't know' argument is the weakest possible form of moral and intellectual argument in human history. It is employed when the truth cannot be admitted because accountability will come into place, and when the lie cannot be successfully marketed" (pg. 109–111). The establishment won't answer Jesus because they can't get away with lying and they won't submit to the truth. There is nothing new under the sun!

Jesus replies, *"Neither will I tell you by what authority I am doing these things."* Jesus has His answer. The religious establishment is unwilling to deal honestly with Him. The fig tree is all leaves and no fruit. So He tells an anti-establishment parable that makes them out to be murderers and thieves. Eventually, they will be overthrown and replaced. He closes the story quoting a messianic reference in Psalm 118 (the song the people were singing at His rally two days before), *"Haven't you read this passage of Scripture: 'The stone the builders rejected has become the cornerstone; the Lord has done this, and it is marvelous in our eyes'?"* Jesus is saying they will reject Him, but the Lord will have the last word.

The elites want to arrest Jesus on the spot because they know He has told this story against them. But they don't touch Him. They are afraid of what the crowd might do to them if they try anything. So they try another question. It is the issue that makes or breaks candidates: taxes.

Every debate has to talk about taxes and this one is no different. For this question, the Pharisees and the Herodians (remember they are political enemies) team up because of their mutual fear of this reformer. They are looking to trap Him. They set Him up with flattery and then ask, *"Is it right to pay taxes to Caesar or not? Should we pay or shouldn't we?"*

They think they have Jesus trapped no matter how He answers. If He says "don't pay," the Herodians have Jesus on insurrection and treason against Rome. If He says "pay," the Pharisees have Him on idolatry and can discredit Him in front of the people.

Jesus, never afraid of hard questions, invites them to examine the evidence with Him. *"Bring me a denarius and let me look at it." They brought Him a coin and He asked them, "Whose portrait [image] is this? And whose inscription?"* On the coin is an image of Tiberius Caesar and on the back it is inscribed, "Tiberius Caesar, son of the divine Augustus." When Jesus asks about the portrait, or "image" in the Greek language, a Jewish mind would immediately think of Genesis 1:27, *"So God created man in His own image, in the image of God He created him; male and female He created them."*

The obvious and only answer to Jesus' question as to whose portrait is on the coin is "Caesar's." That is how they reply. *"Then Jesus said to them, 'Give to Caesar what is Caesar's and to God what is God's.'"* In other words, as Rankin writes, "If Caesar is so foolish to call himself a god and circulate a coin that says so, then give him back his portrait and his folly. But most importantly, give God back His portrait—which is not our money inscribed with the name of a pretender, but our souls, which are made in God's image and are His true possession" (*Enemies*, pg. 117–119).

Again, the opposition has no reply. They are stunned into silence. As Jesus flips the coin back to them I wonder what hits the ground first; the coin or their jaws.

Next up are the Sadducees. They are the priestly class. A small but well-funded third-party group that controls the Temple and its operations. While they hold influence in the Jewish ruling class, they are a minority that does not hold to all the orthodox teaching of the scriptures. In these debates, they see a chance to move to the top of the heap if they can stump Jesus. They ask a question about marriage and the resurrection. They quote Moses and then concoct a ridiculous situation to illustrate their point that the resurrection is for the uneducated. It is a hypothetical question in which they try to show how smart they are. Unfortunately for them, they come across as policy wonks and end up looking foolish.

For starters, they ask a question about the resurrection, a doctrine they deny. (Remember, resurrection is a major plank in the party platform Jesus has laid out.) So Jesus calls them out on it. He tells them they are flat wrong. *"Are you not in error because you do not know the scriptures or the power of God."* He answers their hypothetical about marriage and then goes right after their error on the resurrection. *"Now about the dead rising—have you not read in the book of Moses, in the account of the bush, how God said to him, 'I am the God of*

Abraham, the God of Isaac, and the God of Jacob? He is not the God of the dead, but the living. You are badly mistaken." Jesus lets them know that God did not say, "I was the God of Abraham, Isaac, and Jacob," but "I am." Abraham, Isaac, and Jacob are alive in the presence of God, who transcends time and space, waiting to be resurrected. Jesus has called out their error and they have nothing more to say.

We finally come to the Town Hall portion of the debate. A question from the crowd comes from a teacher of the Law, a Pharisee, who has been watching Jesus answer well. He wants to know which commandment is the most important. Jesus answers, *"Love the Lord your God with all your heart, and with all your soul, and with all your mind, and with all your strength. The second is this: Love your neighbor as yourself. There is no command greater than these."*

This man from the crowd agrees with Jesus and affirms His interpretation of the Law. And then Jesus says something rare to him. *"You are not far from the kingdom of God."* The only thing left for this guy to do is to cast his vote for Jesus to be Messiah. But would he be able to give up his elite status and become an outsider as well?

"And from then on no one dared ask Him any more questions." Jesus has welcomed all questions and given honest answers. He took their hardest questions and they silenced themselves on the issues. He dominated the debates. But He is not done yet. He has one more question that brings it all full circle, back to the question about His authority.

"How is it that the teachers of the law say that the Christ (Messiah) *is the son of David? David himself, speaking by the Holy Spirit, declared: 'The Lord said to my Lord: "Sit at my right hand until I put your enemies under your feet."' David himself calls him 'Lord.' How can he be his son?"*

What is Jesus saying? He is quoting Psalm 110:1, the most quoted or referenced Old Testament verse in the New Testament. The Messiah is more than just a descendant of David. David would never call a descendant "my Lord." But David would call the Son of God, "my Lord." And God has seated the Messiah at His right hand giving Him all authority and power. Jesus is revealing who He is and where He gets His authority.

His final remarks include a warning about the teachers of the law and how fake they are. The large crowd is delighted with what He is saying and the polls show Him the clear winner. But winning the debates and winning the election are two different things. Especially, when your platform is about losing.

Discussion Questions:

1. What do you remember about past presidential debates?
2. Have you ever wanted to ask a question during one of those debates?
3. Do you think Jesus is afraid of hard questions? Why or why not?
4. What do you think of Dr. John Rankin's explanation of the "I don't know" argument? Have you ever seen a politician use it? Is Rankin right?
5. Many people think Jesus is separating church and state with His answer on taxes. Is He or is He communicating something else?
6. Would you say Jesus won the debates? Why or why not?
7. How would you answer Jesus' final question from Psalm 110:1? How can the Messiah be David's son? Whose son is the Messiah?
8. If you could ask Jesus a question, what would it be?

Predicting Doom and Gloom

Mark 13:1–14:11

Civilization will end within fifteen or thirty years unless
immediate action is taken against problems facing mankind.
—George Wald,
Harvard Biologist, Earth Day, 1970

As they leave the Temple, the disciples must have been thinking about victory. They are looking at the buildings, perhaps trying to decide where their office is going to be. Jesus has just demolished the opposition on their own turf. That turf would soon be theirs! In their enthusiasm they say, *"Look Teacher! What massive stones! What magnificent buildings!"*

And Jesus does it again. He rains on their power parade. *"Do you see all these great buildings?"* replied Jesus. *"Not one stone will be left on another, everyone will be thrown down."* The disciples are silent as they walk through the Kidron Valley to the Mount of Olives east of Jerusalem. Sitting on the mount looking at the Temple, they ask Jesus when these things are going to happen and how will they know ahead of time.

Jesus begins by warning them that there will be plenty of false messiahs running for office. History will continue as it always has. Nations and kingdoms will go to war in the quest for power and dominance, but don't be alarmed by such reports. *"These are the beginning of the birth pangs."* The end is still to come.

In case the disciples think they are going to have corner offices in the new administration, Jesus reminds them of what they can expect as they follow the party platform. *"You will be handed over to the local councils and flogged in synagogues. On account of me you will stand before governors and kings as witnesses to them. And the gospel must first be preached to all the nations."*

What are they to be witnesses of before governors and kings? Why must the gospel be preached to all nations? What is the gospel again? The kingdom of God is near. Telling that to governors and kings may not be good news to them. It means their kingdom and power is at an end. No wonder Jesus goes on to explain what to do when they are arrested, betrayed by family members, and hated by all men. Treason has that effect. But He tells them to stand firm and persevere.

But half way through the conversation, Jesus changes tactics and tells them when it will be time to run. Remember, the question was about the destruction of the Temple in Jerusalem, not the end of the world. When that destruction takes place it will be so bad He doesn't want his friends anywhere near it. What is the sign that they should run? N. T. Wright explains, "He is talking about the moment when foreign armies will take over the Temple. We, with historical hindsight, know how this happened in AD 70. We can read, in the historian Josephus, the terrible tale of the siege of Jerusalem; how people starved, ate their own babies to stay alive, fought each other both for scraps of dirty food and for small-scale political gains in factional fighting, more Jews being killed by other Jews than by the invading Romans. Jesus clearly wanted His followers to get out and run. There was no place for misguided national loyalty, for staying to the bitter end of that appalling time" (*Mark for Everyone*, pg. 182).

Even today, candidates make predictions of what will happen should they lose the election. For their followers, it seems like the end of the world. November 9, 2016, had a lot of doom and gloom, end of the world rhetoric. You could almost hear from media pundits, "the sun will be darkened, and the moon will not give its light; the stars will fall from the sky, and the heavenly bodies will be shaken."

And as the Temple collapses, the center of Jewish life and identity, so does their world. What would become the center for life and identity afterwards? *"At that time men will see the Son of Man coming in the clouds with great power and glory. And He will send His angels and gather His elect from the four winds, from the ends of the earth to the ends of the heavens."*

"In Daniel 7 itself, this is not about the **return** of the 'son of man,' but about his 'coming' *to* God after suffering. It is about judgment falling on the system that has opposed God's call and God's gospel; and about Israel's representative sitting down, as David's Lord does in Psalm 110, at God's right hand. From Jesus' point of view, in other words it concerns that vindication of his entire programme and mission which God will bring to pass, after his own death, with the destruction of the Temple that has come to symbolize all that his gospel opposes. From Mark's point of view, it is about complete vindication of Jesus: his resurrection, his ascension, and the outworking of his prophecies against the Temple as sealing the whole process" (Wright, pg. 184).

Jesus tells His disciples that all of this (the destruction of the Temple and the vindication of the Son of Man) will happen within their generation. He adds, *"Heaven and earth will pass away, but my words will never pass away."* What does this mean for political kingdoms, kings, nations, and governments? Have they just been term-limited?

He concludes by telling them, *"No one knows about that day or hour, not even the angels in heaven, nor the Son, but only the Father. Be on guard! Be alert! You do not know when the time will come."* This advice would soon be neglected.

Later at a dinner party, Jesus makes another prediction about the destruction of a different temple. A woman carrying a very expensive jar of perfume interrupts the meal. She breaks the jar open and pours the perfume on Jesus' head. It seems she understands better than His campaign staff how close the platform is to being fully implemented.

They can't see beyond what could have been a nice puff piece in the press and indignantly react to the waste. They reason the perfume could have been sold for a year's wages and the money given to the poor. It is a missed PR moment and they begin to let her know it.

But Jesus doesn't see it that way. *"Leave her alone,"* said Jesus. *"Why are you bothering her? She has done a beautiful thing to me. The poor you will always have with you, and you can help them any time you want. But you will not always have me. She did what she could. She poured perfume on my body beforehand to prepare for my burial. I tell you the truth, wherever the gospel is preached throughout the world, what she has done will also be told in memory of her."*

This is the breaking point for Judas. Apparently, being so close to victory, he is tired of all this talk about losing. He has seen the polls. He knows Jesus is the crowd favorite. If He won't fight, perhaps the crowd will. All they need is a little push. Once they see the establishment move against Jesus, they will revolt. Jesus will have to take action and defend Himself. So Judas makes a deal with the chief priests to betray Jesus. All that is necessary is the opportune moment.

Discussion Questions:

1. Give some recent examples of "end of the world" political rhetoric.
2. Was Jesus' prediction of the destruction of the Temple accurate?
3. Why would it be considered treasonous to preach the Gospel? Under what forms of government is it illegal to do so today? Why?
4. Mark 13:31 Jesus says, "Heaven and earth will pass away, but my words will never pass away." What does this mean for kingdoms, kings, political parties, nations, governments? What does this mean concerning Jesus' candidacy?
5. What is the end result of birth pangs?

6. If your Temple was destroyed, what would be the center for your life and identity?
7. How do we neglect being on guard and alert today? For what should we be on guard and alert?
8. What is Jesus predicting in response to the woman's action at the dinner party?
9. Why do you think Judas agrees to betray Jesus?

THE ELECTION

---•---

Mark 14:12–16:8

A man with God is always in the majority.

—John Knox

ELECTION NIGHT

---·•·---

Mark 14:12–31

Dear Jack: Don't buy a single vote more than necessary.
I'll be damned if I'm going to pay for a landslide.
—John F. Kennedy reading a
telegram from his father
at the Gridiron Club Dinner, 1958

It has been an exciting campaign. Jesus declared His candidacy for Messiah and stormed across the country with His stump speech, *"The time has come, the Kingdom of God is near. Repent and believe the good news."* His campaign rallies were always packed. He was clearly the people's choice. He got the nomination and laid out His losing platform, that He must suffer, be rejected by the establishment, be killed, and after three days rise again. He won the debates as His opponents silenced themselves. Now it is time to vote. Who do you say Jesus is? Election night is here.

Election night in America is always a wild ride. It is full of anticipation, predictions, interviews, and results. Media pundits talk endlessly about the possibilities as polls close across the time zones and vote totals become official. Election night 2000 left the country in limbo for weeks as recount after recount took place in Florida. Election officials tried to determine if a hanging chad was an official vote or not. The Supreme Court finally had to stop the chaos and George W. Bush was declared the winner.

Yet nothing could have prepared the country for the surprise of Election Night 2016. Every expert, every insider, and every pundit thought Hillary Clinton was going to become the first female president. All the polls had Donald Trump losing. When the sun rose the next morning, the impossible had happened. The establishment was in shock for years afterwards.

As the evening begins, Jesus is at His headquarters with His friends preparing for what is going to be a long night. Momentum is clearly in His favor as they celebrate with a meal. Within the last week crowds had packed every Jesus venue and He was victorious at the debates. Everyone is excited and optimistic when Jesus begins to predict the exit polls. *"I tell you the truth, one of you will betray me— one who is eating with me."*

Talk about wrecking the moment! Shock overwhelms the group. Who would do such a thing? And why? The mood gets serious quickly as each one of His disciples says, *"Surely not I?"* Before they can get their heads wrapped around what He is saying, Jesus adds that it is one of His inner circle. One who had shared in the campaign, seen all the miracles, walked the trail, even carried the message. *"The Son of Man will go just as it is written about Him. But woe to that man who betrays the Son of Man! It would be better for him if he had not been born."* No one in the room knows what to do with that.

Then Jesus begins to flesh out His losing platform. *"While they were eating, Jesus took bread, gave thanks and broke it, and gave it to His disciples, saying, 'Take it; this is my body.' Then He took the cup, gave thanks and offered it to them, and they all drank from it. 'This is my blood of the new covenant, which is poured out for many. I tell you the truth, I will not drink again from the fruit of the vine until that day I drink it anew in the Kingdom of God.'"*

A broken body and His blood poured out? This doesn't sound like winning. It sounds like a slaughter.

After that they need some fresh air so they leave the headquarters and head to the garden. On the way Jesus continues to predict the results. They are not good. *"You will all fall away for it is written: 'I will strike the shepherd and the sheep will be scattered.' But after I have risen I will go ahead of you into Galilee."*

Peter, wanting to stop the downward spiral, answers Jesus, *"Even if all fall away, I will not."* Jesus responds with another prediction, *"I tell you the truth, today—yes, tonight—before the rooster crows twice you yourself will disown me three times."* Peter doesn't believe what he is hearing. He loses his cool and insists, *"Even if I have to die with you, I will never disown you."* And everyone else joins him in that sentiment.

But Peter and the rest blew right by it. Didn't anyone hear the words *"after I have risen"*? They are so emphatic to express their will and desire in the matter that they miss what Jesus is saying is going to happen. How true is that of you? Are you so determined to get God to do your will in an election, so hell bent to tell Him how things have to go, that you miss what He is doing? We put our faith and hope in people, politicians, parties, and government programs to solve our problems instead of trusting the One who actually rules the heavens and the earth. It is called idolatry and it destroys people and nations, no matter what their politics are.

People complain about the loss of civility in American politics and rightfully so. I believe the rancor we see in our nation is a direct result of putting our faith and trust in people and parties, rather than God. When our politician, party, or ideology loses then our hope is gone. Our god lost. Our sense of justice and righteousness are shattered. Anger, rage, and hopelessness is all that is left. #resist becomes the only option.

But there is another way. Psalm 146:3–10 gives us some great advice that we had better not blow by.

> *Do not put your trust in princes,*
> *in mortal men, who cannot save.*
> *When their spirit departs,* [or their term expires]
> *they return to the ground;*
> *on that very day their plans come to nothing.*

Blessed is he whose help is the God of Jacob,
whose hope is in the LORD his God,
the Maker of heaven and earth,
the sea, and everything in them –
the LORD who remains faithful forever.
He upholds the cause of the oppressed
and gives food to the hungry.
The LORD sets prisoners free,
the LORD gives sight to the blind,
the LORD lifts up those who are bowed down,
the LORD loves the righteous.
The LORD watches over the alien
and sustains the fatherless and the widow,
but He frustrates the ways of the wicked.

The LORD reigns forever,
your God, O Zion, for all generations.

Praise the LORD.

Who or what are you putting your faith and trust in?

Something else to chew on—three times on election night Jesus has started a sentence, *"I tell you the truth."* He does this all throughout His campaign. It is important to consider that this is how He makes His campaign promises. We are so accustomed to campaign promises turning out to be false that to actually see a politician keep one is a shock. Take some time, go back and see how many of the campaign promises Jesus makes are true. Let's see if these three made on election night are kept.

Discussion Questions:

1. What three exit poll predictions does Jesus make? Are they accurate?
2. Have you ever been so busy telling God how things should go that you miss what He is actually doing?

3. What does idolatry look like in our country today?
4. What do you think is the cause of the loss of civility in our political discourse?
5. Who or what are you putting your faith and trust in for a better world?
6. How does Truth factor into all of this? Who gets to decide what is true?

THE VOTE

Mark 14:32–15:20

I never voted for anybody. I always voted against.
—W. C. Fields

They arrive at the garden and Jesus is at the breaking point. The thought of His closest friends betraying and abandoning Him compounded with His impending suffering and death is too much. His soul is overwhelmed. He asks His friends to pray for Him. Going off by Himself in the garden, *"He fell to the ground and prayed that if possible the hour might pass from Him."* Jesus desires a different platform. *"Abba, Father, everything is possible for You. Take this cup from me."* And then Jesus casts the first vote. *"Yet not what I will, but what You will."* Jesus votes for suffering, rejection, death, and resurrection.

Then it all starts happening just as Jesus promised. The voting begins. Judas arrives with a crowd of soldiers armed with clubs and swords. He goes up to Jesus and votes against Him with a kiss. The soldiers arrest Jesus and His disciples vote with their feet. They desert Him and run away.

Jesus is brought before the Sanhedrin, the establishment's ruling council made up of Pharisees, Sadducees, chief priests, elders, and teachers of the law. They are the super delegates. Jesus is put through a rigged trial. The Sanhedrin is not interested in finding the

74

truth, but only evidence to convict Jesus and put Him to death. The outcome has been predetermined. They have no evidence. Witnesses come forward and accuse Jesus of threatening to destroy the Temple and build another in three days, yet they cannot get their statements to agree. Throughout this whole sham, Jesus doesn't say a word.

Finally, the high priest asked Him, *"Are you the Christ, the Son of the Blessed One?"*

This is what the entire campaign has been about.

For the first time during His trial, He answers. *"I am. And you will see the Son of Man sitting at the right hand of the Mighty One and coming on the clouds of heaven."*

Boom! This is a bombshell moment!

Jesus has just combined a claim to divinity and two Messianic passages from Scripture to answer that question. He does not want to leave any doubt. To begin with, you don't say *"I am."* That's the translation of the name of the Lord, Yahweh. It is the name the Lord told Moses at the burning bush. By saying *"I am"* in that context, Jesus is equating Himself with God. And for good measure He also throws in a reference from Psalm 110 about sitting at the right hand of God and one from Daniel 9:7 about the Son of Man coming on the clouds with power and authority. These references are not lost on His audience.

The high priest tears his clothes and cries out, *"Blasphemy!"* No more need for witnesses. The trial is over. This is all they need for a death sentence. The high priest calls for a vote. It is unanimous. They vote to condemn Jesus. They spit on Him and strike Him with their fists. The guards beat Him. The party platform is being implemented.

Meanwhile, outside in the courtyard, Peter has been denying any association with Jesus because of the pressure brought by a servant girl. Three times he claims not to know Jesus. It is not until the rooster crows that Peter realizes how he has voted. He breaks down and weeps.

Early the next morning, the Sanhedrin take Jesus to the Roman governor, Pilate. There must have been some conversation as to why they are there because Pilate asks Jesus, *"Are you the king of the Jews?"* Jesus answers, *"Yes, it is as you say."* He is not being vague about who He is. Within the last few hours, Jesus has claimed to be the Messiah or Christ, the Son of God, and now, the king of the Jews. It appears Jesus thinks if everyone gets a vote, everyone should be an informed voter.

The chief priests continue to accuse Jesus of many things before Pilate, but Jesus makes no reply. This amazes Pilate. It also leaves him in a bit of a predicament. Pilate has to make a decision as to whether Jesus should be executed. He has to vote but he doesn't like his options. He has found no crime in Jesus, just accusations. He wants to wash his hands of the whole thing so he does what most politicians do. Pilate leaves the decision to the crowd.

This is where the establishment gets a face. They now have their candidate. His name is Barabbas. He is an insurrectionist and murderer. It is interesting that their candidate is guilty of the very thing of which they accuse Jesus. But hypocrisy is the least of their concerns. The establishment doesn't care who they run as their candidate. He or she can be as corrupt as a three-dollar bill so long as they get to keep their power and position. They stir up the crowd to vote against Jesus.

Pilate asks, *"Do you want me to release to you the king of the Jews?"* The crowd shouted their vote for Barabbas. *"What shall I do, then, with the one you call the king of the Jews?"* The establishment doesn't allow opponents like this to mount another campaign. They have to be taken out. The crowd shouts back, *"Crucify Him!"* Pilate asks, *"Why? What crime has He committed?"* But they shouted all the louder, *"Crucify Him!"*

"Wanting to satisfy the crowd, Pilate released Barabbas to them. He had Jesus flogged and handed Him over to be crucified." The crowd votes to lift up Jesus on a cross. Did you notice that Pilate doesn't vote? He doesn't want to get his hands dirty in the whole thing. Lots of people don't vote. They don't want to participate in the process

because politics is dirty and they want to be above it all. Yet their abstention has consequences. Pilate doesn't vote and now the people have a murderer in their midst instead of a healer. Not voting is voting.

The Roman soldiers have a chance to vote. They vote to put a purple robe on Jesus and give Him a crown of thorns. They shout out, *"Hail, king of the Jews!"* They beat Jesus. They hit Him on the head with a staff again and again. They fall on their knees in homage to Him. *"And when they had mocked Him, they took off the purple robe and put His own clothes on Him. Then they led Him out to be crucified."*

Discussion Questions:

1. Are you surprised at the voting results?
2. How is not voting still voting?
3. For what is Jesus condemned? Is it political? If not, then what?
4. Why do you think the crowd votes against Jesus after rejoicing as He rode into Jerusalem less than a week before?
5. Is there anyone who has not voted yet?

THE ELECTION RESULTS

Mark 15:21–16:8

"Dewey Defeats Truman"
(front page headline, *Chicago Daily Tribune*, November 3, 1948).

It is turning into a landslide for the establishment and a massacre for Jesus. He is nailed to a cross. The election is over. The exit polls are mockingly posted above His head, *"King of the Jews."* Jesus lost just as He said He would. The news media jumps into the fray hurling insults and deriding Jesus for His campaign promises. *"So! You who were going to destroy the temple and build it in three days, come down from the cross and save yourself."* The talking heads go on to explain how His campaign fell apart. They walk back through the ups and downs of the campaign. *"He saved others, but He can't save himself! Let this Christ, this King of Israel, come down now from the cross that we may see and believe."* Even those crucified next to Jesus get in on the insults.

With only a few breaths left, Jesus cries out, *"My God, my God, why have you forsaken me?"* It appears, even after the endorsements, God votes against Jesus. And with a loud cry of suffering, after being rejected and beaten, Jesus dies.

Nobody voted for Jesus, but Jesus. His friends abandoned Him. His countrymen handed Him over to a foreign power. He was put through a sham of a trial by the establishment on trumped up charges. He was denied justice and lost, just like He promised. He got one vote—His own.

It is not until after He dies that people begin to vote for Him. The first votes Jesus gets are from those who saw Him die. *"And when the centurion, who stood in front of Jesus heard His cry and saw how He died, he said, 'Surely this man was the Son of God!'"* Several women, Mary Magdalene and others, who had followed Jesus and cared for His needs during the campaign, are watching all of this. He gets their votes. Joseph of Arimathea, a prominent council member who himself is waiting for the kingdom of God to come, takes Jesus' body down from the cross and places it in a proper tomb. He votes for Jesus.

But what good are their votes now? Jesus is dead and buried. A large stone seals the entrance to the tomb. All His promises of hope and change, of restoration, of the kingdom of God coming are as lifeless as He is. But the swing vote is yet to come. Remember, there is still one more plank in the platform that needs to be implemented.

Early Sunday morning the women go to the tomb to anoint the body of Jesus. They are worried about the stone blocking the entrance to the tomb when their whole world is rocked. The stone is rolled back. They enter the tomb and discover Jesus is not there. There is a man dressed in a white robe and he delivers the election results. *"Don't be alarmed! You're looking for Jesus the Nazarene who was crucified. He is risen! He's not here."*

The only vote that matters has been cast. God votes for Jesus by raising Him from the dead! With this one vote, God has vindicated Jesus and everything He has said about Himself in the campaign! Jesus has fulfilled the whole platform, even the last plank—resurrection!

The women leave the tomb scared and confused. The earliest manuscripts of Mark end with the women saying nothing to anyone. It is a weird way to end his book. It's as if Mark is waiting for your vote.

So, what is your vote? Who do you say Jesus is? Is He the Christ, the Messiah, the Son of God, the King of the Jews? Is Jesus the Lord of all or is Jesus just another failed candidate? Each of us gets a vote—and remember, not voting is a vote. How do you vote?

Now just because God gives each of us a vote doesn't mean God is going to tally them up, check for hanging chads, and declare a winner. Our vote has an outcome for us, but it does not determine the outcome of this election. God holds the only vote that determines the outcome and, truth be told, it was never in question.

Psalm 2 gives us the election results before the campaign even began.

Why do the nations conspire
and the peoples plot in vain?
The kings of the earth take their stand
and the rulers gather together
against the LORD
and against his Anointed One.
"Let us break off their chains," they say,
"and throw off their fetters."
The One enthroned in heaven laughs;
the Lord scoffs at them.
Then he rebukes them in his anger
and terrifies them in his wrath,
saying,
"I have installed my King
on Zion, my holy hill."

I will proclaim the decree of the LORD:

He said to me, "You are my Son;
today I have become your Father.
Ask of me,
and I will make the nations your inheritance,
the ends of the earth your possession.

You will rule them with an iron scepter;
You will dash them to pieces like pottery."

Therefore, you kings, be wise;
be warned, you rulers of the earth.
Serve the LORD with fear
and rejoice with trembling.
Kiss the Son, lest he be angry
and you be destroyed in your way,
for His wrath can flare up in a moment.
Blessed are all who take refuge in Him.

Jesus is King of heaven and earth. This is what the scriptures have always declared, are still declaring, and will continue to declare forever! Jesus has run for the highest office and won. The Hope of the world is not found in a current political candidate on either side of the aisle. God has made Jesus both Lord and Christ. He is the King and His kingdom has no term limit.

The Kingdom of God is not a spiritual kingdom in the afterlife that has little or no implications for earthly life. The righteous governing of humanity has always been the business of a just and loving God. His kingdom reunites heaven and earth as Jesus, the King of kings, rules all the nations with dominion and power forever. His rule restores everything to the original creation plan where the lion lays down with the lamb; love and faithfulness meet together; righteousness and peace kiss each other; justice rolls down like a mighty water; and God dwells with humanity. His reign will make creation great again. There is a new day coming and here is what it looks like:

"Now the dwelling of God is with men, and he will live with them. They will be his people, and God himself will be with them and be their God. He will wipe away every tear from their eyes. There will be no more death or mourning or crying or pain, for the old order of things has passed away" (Rev. 21:3–4).

The old order has been passing away since the women ran from the empty tomb with the Good News. I know it sounds crazy, even foolish, to believe that Jesus of Nazareth is Lord over Washington,

New York, Rio de Janeiro, London, Paris, Cairo, Nairobi, Moscow, Beijing, Seoul, Tokyo, Sydney, and every other place on the planet, especially, Jerusalem. I realize it makes no sense how a man crucified between two thieves is King of the universe. I get that it is a stumbling block for many to accept that God raised Jesus from the dead. But crazy, foolish, or a stumbling block doesn't make it untrue.

The plan all along has been for Jesus to turn the world right side up. With the world being wrong side up anything Jesus does or says might look foolish and weak. *"But God chose the foolish things of the world to shame the wise; God chose the weak things of the world to shame the strong. He chose the lowly things of this world and the despised things—and the things that are not—to nullify the things that are, so that no one may boast before Him" (1 Cor. 1:27–29).*

Friends, THE campaign is over. No matter who wins the next election, Jesus is still Lord. You can continue to give your allegiance and trust to other candidates who promise "hope and change" or to "make America great again." But in the end you will be left disappointed. Only Jesus can deliver.

Cast your vote for Jesus. Give your allegiance and trust to Him. Join His party and spread the message:

The time has come.
The Kingdom of God is near.
Repent and believe the Good News!

Discussion Questions:

1. Why does it seem God votes against Jesus?
2. With His final breaths, Jesus prays the first line of Psalm 22. Clearly this Psalm is on His mind. If verses 1–21 describe His crucifixion, what do verses 22–31 describe?
3. When do people begin to vote for Jesus? Do their votes change the outcome?

4. Whose vote determines the outcome of the election? How is it cast?
5. What does your vote determine?
6. How do you vote? Is Jesus Lord?

THE TRANSITION

Mark 16:9-20

Go into all the world and preach the good news to all creation.

—*Jesus*

The immediate reaction of those who have been with Jesus from the beginning of the campaign as they hear the results of the election is disbelief. That is the case as Mary Magdalene, the first to see Jesus alive, tells the others. They do not believe her. When two other people come in with news that they have seen Jesus alive, they are not believed either. Even today, most people who hear that Jesus is risen from the dead and is now Lord over heaven and earth do not believe. Why this reluctancy to believe?

Maybe because this news is unlike anything anyone has heard before. The rule for dead people is that once they die they stay dead. There may be an occasional death and comeback on an operating table. Some people report "near death experiences" where they have died, see the other side and then come back. But death will eventually catch up with them again as well. Who, besides Jesus, can you think of that has beaten death forever? Who's grave is empty for all time? See, hard to believe.

Perhaps another reason people are hesitant to believe this good news is because they don't see any difference in the world. If Jesus is Lord over heaven and earth, what's He doing now? Why is He waiting to implement His kingdom on earth as it is in heaven?

After an election there is always a time of transition. The newly elected are gearing up to take office while the outgoing are wrapping things up. It is an awkward time for everyone involved because power is being transferred from one person or party to another. For a short period of time the incoming president-elect is putting his or her administration in place but does not have any power to officially act. It is not until Inauguration Day when the new president is sworn in and officially has the power and authority to make decisions and act.

So is that the problem? Is Jesus Savior-elect waiting to take His seat of power and begin acting? No, not at all. Jesus is not in transition. Mark tell us in 16:19 *"After the Lord Jesus had spoken to them, He was taken up into heaven and He sat at the right hand of God."* Jesus is not waiting to be crowned or take His seat of authority and power. He has it right now. So then what is His game plan? Why is He waiting to act?

His game plan sounds as crazy today as it did when He first says it to His disciples. They are sitting around not believing the good news themselves, even though eyewitness reports keep coming in to the contrary. Finally, that evening on the first Easter Sunday, Jesus appears to His disciples and rebukes them for their failure to believe He fulfilled the last plank of the party platform. And then He spells out the game plan: *"Go into all the world and preach the good news to all creation."*

The disciples have to be thinking, "You want us to do what? Wouldn't it be more effective if you, Jesus, hit the speaking circuit? You would be more convincing than us. After all, seeing is believing. And the opposition would crumble at Your mere appearance!" Perhaps they are waiting for Peter to take Jesus aside again and explain that to Him. But Peter isn't about to repeat what happened at the convention.

No, the game plan is for the disciples, the people who voted for Jesus, to go into the whole world and share the good news that He has won. For some weird reason Jesus wants us to participate in bringing in His rule and reign across the globe. Granted He could do it all by Himself, but He is giving us the privilege of sharing in His glory. He tells His disciples not only are they to preach the good news, but that

He will exercise His power and authority through them. He says, *"Whoever believes and is baptized will be saved, but whoever does not believe will be condemned. And these signs will accompany those who believe: In my name they will drive out demons; they will speak in new tongues; they will pick up snakes with their hands; and when they drink deadly poison, it will not hurt them at all; they will place their hands on sick people, and they will get well."*

These signs are the Kingdom coming on earth as it is in heaven. Joining Christ's party means you get to participate in Kingdom work! Paul will go so far in 2 Corinthians 5:20 as to call those who have joined His party *"Christ's ambassadors."*

I know many people who watch news reports day after day and all they get from it is fear. The world continues to fall apart and solutions from elected leaders around the world don't work. How desperate they are for good news and we have it! Jesus is Lord! He has addressed the root issue and provided a real solution at the cross. He has overcome sin, death, and hell. And He offers everlasting life to those who put their trust in Him. This is good news indeed! In this partisan world where everything has been politicized, people need to hear the good news that Jesus is victorious and reigning forever. We get the privilege of being heralds for the King.

But it comes with a cost. We will encounter opposition in the same way Jesus did. Remember, those in power do not like to have their power challenged, much less told it is in transition. It is fading away and will not prevail. We will encounter demons, snakes, and poison. (This is politics after all.) The opposition will do everything it can to deny the truth of Jesus' victory. They will spread fake news that it couldn't happen, didn't happen, or that only fools believe it. They will trumpet crisis after crisis and offer themselves or their party's ideology as the only solution.

But they will not be victorious. Instead, as we preach the good news, the signs of His kingdom and rule will continue to break into this world. People will be healed. Demons will be cast out. More and more people will be brought out of fear and darkness and receive a living hope and everlasting life. That is the transition. All of creation will be set free from the bondage of sin and death into the glorious freedom, peace, righteousness and joy of the kingdom of God.

As we go into the whole world and preach the good news it will be incumbent upon those of us who have joined His party to remember the party platform. *"If anyone would come after me, he must deny himself and take up his cross and follow me. For whoever wants to save his life will lose it, but whoever loses his life for me and for the gospel will save it."*

The party platform is to lose in order to win. His ambassadors are not bent on world domination. We are called upon to take up our cross for the good news. That may mean losing face, arguments, rights, money, position, power, reputation, friends, family, even life itself. The good news we proclaim does not force anyone into His kingdom. Jesus always gives us the choice; a vote. He desires that everyone choose to come in by their own free will.

That is another reason why it seems He is waiting to fully implement the kingdom on earth. Peter writes to others years after the resurrection, *"You must understand that in the last days scoffers will come, scoffing and following their own evil desires. They will say, "Where is this 'coming' He promised? Ever since our fathers died, everything goes on as it has since the beginning of creation." But do not forget this one thing, dear friends: With the Lord a day is like a thousand years and a thousand years are like a day. The Lord is not slow in keeping His promise, as some understand slowness. He is patient with you, not wanting anyone to perish, but everyone to come to repentance."* (2 Peter 4:3-4,8-9)

He is waiting because not everyone has had the opportunity to cast a vote. Make no mistake, Jesus is victorious and He is coming back to establish His kingdom completely. But until that day, we are to hit the campaign trail on His behalf regardless of who wins the next election.

The disciples do just that. *"Then the disciples went out and preached everywhere, and the Lord worked with them and confirmed His word by the signs that accompanied it."* Now it is our turn. Those who have voted for Jesus, who have joined His party, are called to go into a partisan world and declare, "This just in: Jesus is still Lord."

Discussion Questions:

1) Why do you think the disciples did not believe the reports of resurrection?

2) Would Jesus rebuke you for your unbelief? Why or why not?

3) How often do you share the good news with others? What would happen if you shared the good news of Jesus the next time a political discussion broke out?

4) What are some signs that this world is in transition and that the Kingdom of God is breaking in?

5) Where will you go to preach the good news?

About the Author

M ichael Hudson is a graduate of Asbury Theological Seminary and pastors a large congregation in Florida. He is grateful to God for his wife and three children. He loves spending time with his family, hiking, reading American history, and traveling. He often wonders how he can have so many friends when his two favorite topics of conversation are religion and politics.

Lightning Source UK Ltd.
Milton Keynes UK
UKHW011144270120
357678UK00004B/1369